I AM ALLOSAURUS

by Timothy J. Bradley

I am *Allosaurus.*

I can hatch.

I am *Allosaurus*.

I can see.

I am *Allosaurus*.

I can run.

I am *Allosaurus*.

I can hide.

I am *Allosaurus.*

I can hunt.

I am *Allosaurus.*

I can eat.

I am *Allosaurus.*

I can grow.

I am *Allosaurus*.

I can see.

I am *Allosaurus.*

I can run.

I am *Allosaurus.*

I can smell.

I am *Allosaurus.*

I can hunt.

I am *Allosaurus.*

I can eat.

I am *Allosaurus*.

I am extinct.

For Creative Minds

About *Allosaurus*

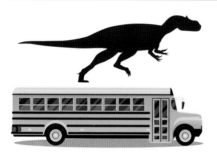

Allosaurus (al-oh-SORE-us) was a dinosaur that lived very long ago. *Allosaurus* was large, growing to about 9 meters (30 feet) long. That is almost as long as a school bus!

Although it was so large, *Allosaurus* may have been a swift hunter, preying on smaller creatures, and possibly some of the larger dinosaurs it shared the world with, like *Stegosauru*s (steg-oh-SORE-us) and *Camarasaurus* (KAM-uh-ruh-SORE-us).

It may also have been a scavenger (SCAV-en-jer), eating already-dead animals. *Allosaurus* may have hunted alone, or possibly in a group.

Scientists now believe that many young dinosaurs had hair-like feathers. The big question is whether the adults had feathers or if the feathers fell out as the dinosaurs grew up. In today's world, birds are the only animals that have feathers. Some flightless birds like the emu and kiwi have hair-like feathers similar to what scientists think the dinosaurs had!

Allosaurus   *Camarasaurus*   *Stegosaurus*

Timeline & Location

Allosaurus

Ceratosaurus

Brachiosaurus

Allosaurus lived 155 to 150 million years ago, during a time called the Jurassic (joor-AS-ik) Period. *Allosaurus* lived after the most primitive dinosaurs, but long before *Tyrannosaurus* (tie-RAN-oh-SORE-us) and *Triceratops* (try-SERR-uh-tops).

Dinosaurs like the predator *Ceratosaurus* (serr-AT-oh-SORE-us) and the giant long-necked *Brachiosaurus* (Brach-ee-oh-SORE-us) lived in the Jurassic world of *Allosaurus*.

The world of *Allosaurus* was different from our world today. Allosaurus lived long before there were any people on Earth. Although you would recognize some of that past world, things that we see around us every day, like grass and flowers, did not yet exist.

Fossil traces of *Allosaurus* have been found in North America, mostly in Wyoming, Colorado and Utah with some found in Montana, South Dakota and New Mexico. *Can you find those states on the map, below? Do you live anywhere near there?*

Allosaurus fossils have also been found in Portugal and scientist may have found one in Tanzania!

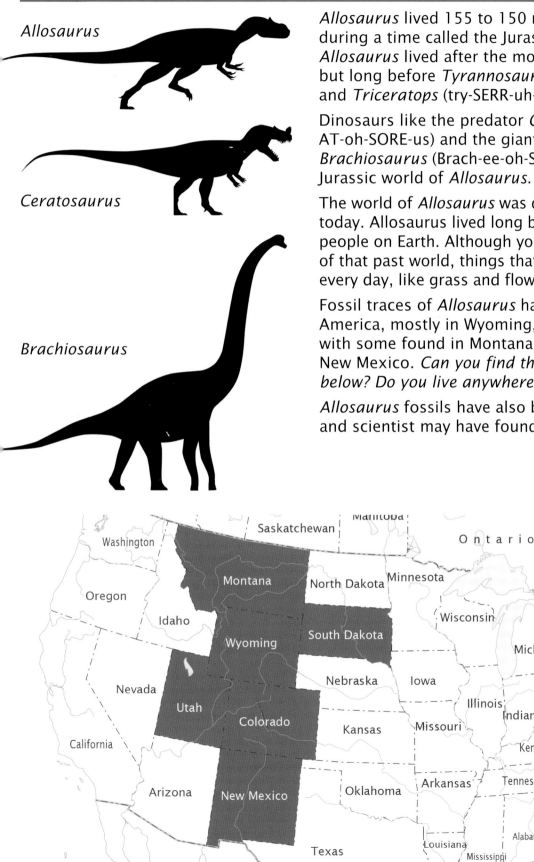

Allosaurus Skeleton and Restoration

Allosaurus comes from the Greek "allos" that means different and "saurus" that means lizard. In other words, the name means "different lizard" because the first skeleton found was so different than any other known dinosaur at the time. Scientists can learn a lot about dinosaurs based on fossils and skeletons that are found.

Allosaurus were large, theropod dinosaurs that walked on two feet (bipedal).

Some of the *Allosaurus*' vertebrae were hollow, just like modern birds. The bones of *Allosaurus* show the long tail that balanced its body. The leg bones of Allosaurus were strong, and may indicate that *Allosaurus* was a large, but swift dinosaur.

Fossilized skulls show large eye sockets and horns above and in front of the eyes. The horns may have acted as "display." The skull of *Allosaurus* had several large holes in it, which may have lightened its weight.

Its teeth were shaped to slice through the flesh of its prey. The front and back of each tooth was serrated (like a knife) with notches for cutting. Its mouth could open extra-wide to use those sharp teeth. If an *Allosaurus* lost a tooth, it would grow a new tooth back. The shape and type of teeth tell scientists that the *Allosaurus* was a carnivore.

The forelimbs, or "arms" were short but were still longer than the T-rex. The hands of *Allosaurus* had three fingers. The thumb was short, with a large claw. The other two fingers were slimmer, with smaller, sharp claws.

The restoration of *Allosaurus* shows how it may have looked when alive. Muscles and skin have been added over the skeleton by an artist.

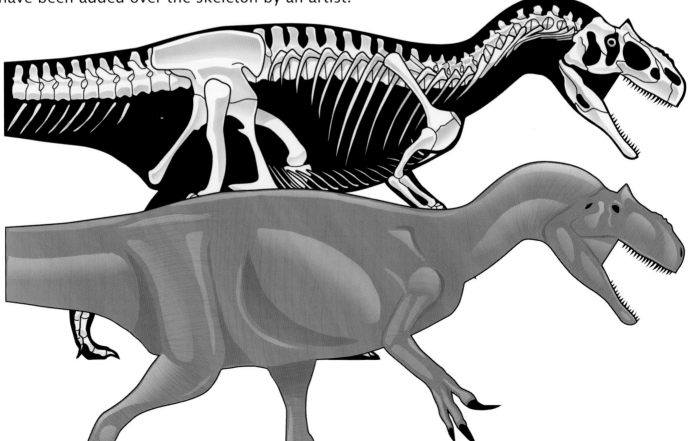

What Colors?

What color was *Allosaurus*? Scientists don't know. Indications of color don't often fossilize, but there have been some clues that show that dinosaurs could see in color, and that they may have had some body parts that were brightly-colored.

Although we can't know for sure what color *Allosaurus* was, it is very possible that it was as brightly-colored as the reptiles and birds we see around us today.

Biologists know that some animals today use bright colors to warn other animals to stay away because they are poisonous. Bright colors might also be used to attract mates. And animals often use colors or patterns to help them hide (camouflage) from predators or prey.

The author and illustrator of this book imagines that *Allosaurus* had pink skin. What color do you think they were? Go to the "For Creative Minds'" section on the book's homepage at www.ArbordalePublishing.com to download a coloring page.

What color do YOU think the *Allosaurus* was?

What did its habitat look like?

How did the color help the *Allosaurus* live in its habitat?

For Kayellen—TJB

Thanks to Professor Kevin Padian, Department of Integrative Biology at the University of California, Berkeley and Dr. Kenneth Carpenter, Director, Prehistoric Museum at Utah State University Eastern for verifying the accuracy of the information in this book.

Library of Congress Cataloging-in-Publication Data

Names: Bradley, Timothy J., author.
Title: I am allosaurus / by Timothy J. Bradley.
Description: Mt. Pleasant, SC : Arbordale Publishing, [2020] | Includes
    bibliographical references. | Audience: Ages 3-7 | Audience: Grades K-1
Identifiers: LCCN 2019031848 (print) | LCCN 2019031849 (ebook) | ISBN
    9781643517490 (hardcover) | ISBN 9781643517544 (trade paperback) | ISBN
    9781643517841 (ebook other) | ISBN 9781643517742 (epub)
Subjects: LCSH: Allosaurus--Juvenile literature.
Classification: LCC QE862.S3 B727 2020 (print) | LCC QE862.S3 (ebook) |
    DDC 567.912--dc23
LC record available at https://lccn.loc.gov/2019031848
LC ebook record available at https://lccn.loc.gov/2019031849

Lexile® Level: 80L
key phrases: dinosaurs, *Allosaurus*
Title in Spanish: **Soy un Alosaurio**

Bibliography:
Castro, Joseph. Allosaurus: Fact About the "Different Lizard." LiveScience. March 15, 2016, internet accessed
    March 2019.
Foster, John. 2007. Jurassic West: the Dinosaurs of the Morrison Formation and Their World. Bloomington,
    Indiana: Indiana University Press.
Paul, Gregory S. (1988). "Genus Allosaurus." Predatory Dinosaurs of the World. New York: Simon & Schuster.

Printed in China, November 2019
This product conforms to CPSIA 2008
First Printing

Arbordale Publishing
Mt. Pleasant, SC 29464
www.ArbordalePublishing.com